THE SOUTHERNER'S BOOK OF LISTS

NEVER HITCHHIKE TOO CLOSE
TO KUDZU.

THE SOUTHERNER'S BOOK OF LISTS

By JIM ERSKINE

PELICAN PUBLISHING COMPANY
Gretna 2000

First printing, July 1996
Second printing, October 1997
Third printing, April 1998
Fourth printing, March 2000

*The word "Pelican" and the depiction of a pelican are trademarks
of Pelican Publishing Company, Inc.,
and are registered in the U.S. Patent and Trademark Office.*

Library of Congress Cataloging-in-Publication Data

Erskine, Jim.
    The southerner's book of lists / Jim Erskine.
        p. cm.
    ISBN 1-56554-149-9
    1. Southern States—Humor. I. Title.
PN6231.S64E76 1996
818'.5402—dc20   96-13703
                                                      CIP

Illustrations by the author

Printed in the United States of America
Published by Pelican Publishing Company, Inc.
1000 Burmaster Street, Gretna, Louisiana 70053

To Susan, Randall, Russell, and Jessie—
smack dab in the middle of my heart

THE SOUTHERNER'S 10 COMMANDMENTS

1. Y'all shalt always remember your manners.

2. Y'all shalt make no fuss over yourself.

3. Y'all shalt not sass your mama.

4. Y'all shalt always wonder what your daddy would think.

5. Y'all shalt always talk the way you grow'ed up.

6. Y'all shalt tell no whoppers unless you are in a situation where you are expected to.

7. Y'all shalt demonstrate your great faith by the way you drive.

8. Y'all shalt always clean your plate.

9. Y'all shalt hold kinfolk in high regard, regardless of what you really think of 'em.

10. Y'all shalt always remember where you come from.

STILL MORE SOUTHERN COMMANDMENTS
(that didn't quite make the cut)

Y'all shalt never say "youse guys."

Y'all shalt always stop and pass the time with folks you meet, no matter how busy you are.

Y'all shalt not stray too far from home, in either body or mind.

Y'all shalt not act uppity about how much money you make or what you got.

Y'all shalt remain modest.

Y'all shalt run over at least one armadillo and/or possum in your driving career.

Y'all shalt have at least one pickup truck in the immediate family.

Y'all shalt trust no restaurant menu; remember that tastin' is believing.

Y'all shalt not trust the word of any Yankee over a true Southerner.

Y'all shalt know what chitlins are, whether you've ever gotten near 'em or not.

Y'all shalt take care both where you spit and where you step.

TAKE CARE
WHERE YOU SPIT —
OR STEP!

DISTINCTIVELY SOUTHERN TRAITS
(that set us apart from "Those-Who-Are-Not-From-Here")

THE SOUTH AS A WHOLE IS EQUAL PARTS . . .

beautiful	tough
dangerous	tender
mannerly	friendly
crazy	religious

THE LOAFING BENCH

CHARACTERISTICS
OF A SOUTHERN LADY

strong

tough

gentle

loving

beautiful

powerful

charming

Southern born and bred

mannerly

vain in the best sense

charismatic

willing to volunteer

romantic

able to throw a royal hissy fit

delicate

able to aim objects at males with

fragile

exceeding accuracy

ladylike

able to manage men without seeming to do so

CHARACTERISTICS
OF A SOUTHERN GENTLEMAN

solid

unpretentious

stand-up

mannerly

has good taste

well educated

chivalrous

takes charge

easygoing

witty

sporting

loves the South

loves Southern women

knows who he is

knows his place

Southern born and bred

has a traditional view of women

courageous when necessary

TOP 7 SPORTS OF THE SOUTH

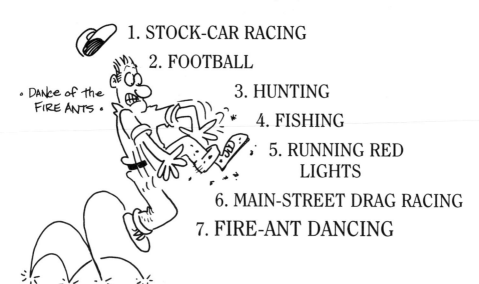

1. STOCK-CAR RACING
2. FOOTBALL
3. HUNTING
4. FISHING
5. RUNNING RED LIGHTS
6. MAIN-STREET DRAG RACING
7. FIRE-ANT DANCING

18 ACCEPTABLE TERMS FOR WHAT YANKEES ERRONEOUSLY REFER TO AS "THE CIVIL WAR"

The Late Misunderstanding

The War

The Uncivil War

The Late Friction

The Late Ruction

The War of Secession

The Yankee Invasion

The War to Suppress Yankee Arrogance

The War for Southern Freedom

The War for Southern Independence

The Second American Revolution

The War for Southern Freedom

The War for States' Rights

The War for Southern Rights

Mr. Lincoln's War

The Great Rebellion

The Lost Cause

BUBBA'S BEST FRIEND
(10 characteristics of the Southern hound dog)

1. Never pure bred.

2. Almost always as ugly as a stick.

3. Usually named Beau, Dog, or Dammit.

4. Snores when he sleeps.

5. Passes large quantities of gas.

6. Able to ride in the back of a pickup truck without falling down.

7. Chases practically anything unless asked to.

8. Barks at everyone and everything but the person breaking into the house.

9. A constant companion and source of understanding for his owner.

10. Usually lives to be 150 in dog years unless he is run over by his owner's wife.

12 CHARACTERISTICS OF SOUTHERN DRIVERS

1. Able to see through several layers of smeared love bugs.

2. Think a yellow light means "put the pedal to the metal."

3. Wave at oncoming drivers whether they know who it is or not.

4. Unable to cruise at or below the speed limit . . . unless they are in the fast lane on the Interstate, where they will often do 40 mph.

5. Always pull over for a funeral procession.

6. Have a weakness for stupid bumper stickers.

7. Drive too close to the car in front of them. (This is due to our closeknit family upbringing.)

8. Sneer at drivers with Northern license tags, unless they happen to be stopping at their place of business.

9. Hate being passed, and will speed up to prevent anyone seeking to do so.

10. Love to pass others and watch them get mad.

11. Will swerve to hit possums, armadillos, and snakes.

12. Slow down to see the hit possums, armadillos, and snakes.

TOP SOUTHERN
VACATION DESTINATIONS

1. Disney World

2. Mardi Gras (New Orleans)

3. Gatlinburg

4. Myrtle Beach

5. Panama City

6. The lake

7. The mountains

8. Opryland

9. Graceland

10. Mama's

TYPICAL SOUTHERN SOUVENIRS

Jack Daniels playing cards

Harley Davidson belt buckles

Stock-car racing T-shirts

Picture postcards of Graceland

Elvis coasters

Country ham by the slice

Ashtray with picture of man in
outhouse with caption: "I'm the only
one in (insert name of state) who
knows what he's doin'."

Boiled peanuts

Stuffed alligator or stuffed frog
playing the banjo

Cypress knees

7 THINGS THAT MAKE YOU MOST ATTRACTIVE TO SOUTHERN INSECTS

1. soft, smooth skin

2. sweat

3. your perfume or cologne

4. dark clothing

5. heat

6. your body, which is a familiar shape that means food to them—much like a 55-gallon barbecue drum is to us

7. your fear of getting bit—which causes you to breathe faster and produce more carbon dioxide, which is downright intoxicating to the pest in question

HOW TO CONVINCE INSECTS TO LEAVE YOU BE

1. wear light-colored clothing to stay cool
2. move and breathe slowly and deliberately
3. use cirtonella candles
4. buy a bug zapper
5. use any bug spray with the ingredient "Deet"
6. or ultimately, as all true Southerners know, accept and ignore them as a small price to pay for living in God's country

FLY SWATTER

SOUTHERN WAYS TO SAY "HELLO"

"Pull up a chair and sit a spell."

"Howzit goin'?"

"What's the news?"

" 'lo."

"So good to see you!"

"Howdy!"

"Well, look at what the cat drug in!"

"Hey there!"

"How's your mama?"

"How y'all doin'?"

"Make yourself to home."

"Workin' hard or hardly workin'?"

"How you folks gettin' along?"

SOUTHERN WAYS TO SAY "YES"
(because "yes" is too obvious a reply)

"You betcha."

"Sho' nuff."

"You got that right."

"I can dance to that."

"You said a mouthful."

"I'm here to tell ya."

"Yes siree, Bob."

"Woooeee . . . you ain't kiddin'."

"You hit the nail on the head."

"Ain't it the truth?"

"Yep."

"Yup."

"Umhum."

"All righty."

"Okey Dokey."

13 WAYS TO SAY GOOD-BYE IN THE SOUTH
(where "good-bye" just won't do)

1. "You boys git along now, hear?"

2. "Y'all stay with us."

3. Spoken to spouse: "Well, let's go on to bed so these good folks can go home."

4. "Come back."

5. "See you real soon."

6. "Y'all sure you can't stay a little bit longer?"

7. "Take care now."

8. (For kinfolk or children) "Git!"

The following actions are also important elements in a proper Southern "good-bye":

9. Wave a lot.

10. Smile big.

11. Keep moving to the door.

12. For those being left: Stand at your front door and wave until the car is out of sight.

13. For those leaving: Wave and honk your horn until out of sight.

11 TRADITIONAL SOUTHERN WAYS TO BEAT THE HEAT
("You can do without air conditioning. The animals do."—Grandma)

1. Hose down the porch and bare your feet.
2. ceiling fans
3. palmetto leaf fans
4. funeral parlor fans
5. soaked quilts hung over open windows
6. Do hot chores (like the laundry) early in the morning—never in the afternoon.

7. iced tea by the gallon

8. fresh-squeezed lemonade

9. shade trees

10. Keep garbage out of smelling range.

11. discreet skinny dipping

JUST WHAT IS THE SOUTH?
(13 common answers to an elusive question)

1. The Confederacy

2. The Confederacy plus Kentucky (and sometimes Maryland)

3. The Confederacy less Texas (a world of its own)

4. Anyplace below the grits line

5. South of the Mason-Dixon Line

6. Everything south of the Mason Dixon Line except Atlanta and southern Florida

7. A state of mind

8. A state of grace

9. Home

10. God's country

11. That area of the country that is overrun with pretty girls, ugly dogs, and dirty pickups

12. Wherever "Y'all" is spoken

13. Wherever natives, when asked if they are Southerners, reply "Hell, yes"

JUST A HANDFUL OF THE HUNDREDS OF BIBLICAL PLACE NAMES THAT CAN BE FOUND IN PRACTICALLY EVERY STATE IN THE SOUTH

Jerusalem	Ninevah	Calvary
Gethsemane	Antioch	Damascus
Canaan	Samaria	Macedonia
Mt. Carmel	Shiloh	Boaz
Mt. Zion	Bethany	Joppa
Bethel	Hebron	Palestine
Sardis	Zion	Ephesus
Ararat		

. . . PLUS 18 MORE SPECIFICALLY-TO-THE-POINT PLACE NAMES
(lest you forget you are squarely in the middle of the Bible Belt)

Preachersville, KY
Temperanceville, VA
Bible Hill, TN
Religion, MS
Churchtown, TN
Baptismal, AL
Seminary, MS
Olive Branch, NC
Church Point, LA
Benevolence, GA

Hopeful, GA
Hymnal, NC
New Hope, GA
Bliss, KY
Providence, AR
Beulahville, NC
Beersheba Springs, TN
and
Hell-For-Certin, KY

BIBLE

9 UNSUNG HEROES OF THE SOUTH
(without whom we wouldn't be who we are)

1. Good waitresses
2. Our Sunday School teacher
3. The preacher
4. The sheriff
5. The owner of the country store
6. Farmers
7. Our grade-school teachers
8. Mama
9. Daddy

10 SOUTHERN ENDEARMENTS
(commonly used to address one's mate, waitress, and dog)

SUGAR PIE

HONEY BUNCH

SWEETIE PIE

PUNKIN'

SUGAR LIPS

HONEY BUN

DUMPLIN'

DARLIN'

SWEET PEA

SUGAR LUMP

12 MOST UNFORGETTABLE SMELLS
OF THE SOUTH
(or, how to tell you're in Dixie even with your eyes closed)

1. barbecue pit
2. fried catfish
3. magnolias in bloom
4. honeysuckle
5. wisteria
6. newly spread pig manure

7. swamp gas

8. wet hound dog

9. tractors (when you are driving behind one on the highway)

10. pole cat

11. paper mill

12. newly mown hay

10 THINGS THAT LET YOU KNOW IT'S NIGHTTIME IN DIXIE

1. the heat
2. the humidity
3. the smell of honeysuckle in the night air
4. june bugs trying to get off their backs on the porch
5. the creak of the porch swing
6. lightning bugs dancing above the yard
7. crickets and katydids drowning out your thoughts
8. the hum of mosquitoes in your ear

9. the hum of an air conditioner

10. the roar of some teenager's souped-up car burning rubber at the red light, then flying down the highway

THE WINDOW AIR CONDITIONER :
ANOTHER UNSUNG HERO OF THE SOUTH

CHICKENS, HEADLESS AND OTHERWISE
(vanishing Southern sights and sounds)

Chickens, headless and otherwise

country general store

kids playing marbles

old men sitting on a bench outside the general store

an old man whittling

pocket watches

homemade toys

Piggly Wiggly stores

the front porch

people actually sitting on the front porch

modestly dressed girls

respectful young people

blushing

boys skinny-dipping in a creek

a mule and plow

dirt roads

bologna sandwiches

peanuts in an RC

fireworks on Christmas

plain white T-shirts

outhouses

BLUSHING

pea fowl

party-line telephones

baton twirling

garden clubs

homemaker clubs

modest bathing suits

families talking together

the Pledge of Allegiance

kids playing leap frog

church homecomings

honeymoon cabins

"See Rock City" signs

HELL FIRE
&
BRIMSTONE

SEERSUCKER
SUITS

CLOSED
SUNDAYS

"Mail Pouch Tobacco" signs
hellfire and brimstone
old-fashioned country music
Saturday kiddie matinees
local radio programming
seersucker suits
family reunions
hula hoops
creek baptisms
big hairdos
saying grace in a restaurant
stores staying closed on a Sunday

22 STRANGE BUT TRUE SOUTHERN LAWS
(travelers beware . . .)

1. It is against the law to sing out of key. (North Carolina)

2. No man may wed his grandmother-in-law. (Kentucky)

3. Drinking milk or water on a train is downright illegal. (North Carolina)

4. Businessmen may not play drums out of doors during lunch time. (Meridian, Mississippi)

5. You will be fined if you milk someone else's cow. (Hattiesburg, Mississippi)

6. No female may appear in a bathing suit on any highway in the Commonwealth of Kentucky, unless escorted by two police officers or she is armed with a club. (*Note:* this law does not apply to females less than 90 pounds or more than 200 pounds.)

7. Wives must have their husband's permission to rearrange household furniture. (Kentucky)

8. No man may wear a topless bathing suit. (Alabama)

9. Males are required to have a valid legal excuse to put their arm around a female. (Macon, Georgia)

10. You are absolutely forbidden to carry any ice-cream cones in your pockets. (Lexington, Kentucky)

11. Dogs are forbidden to bark after sundown. (Little Rock, Arkansas)

12. You will break the law if you purchase a bag of peanuts after sundown. (Alabama)

ILLEGAL ICE CREAM TRANSPORT (LEXINGTON, KY)

13. Any woman wishing to buy a hat must have her husband try it on first. (Kentucky)

14. The wearing of a false mustache in church is illegal. (Alabama)

15. A fisherman may not take any fish off another person's line. (Tennessee)

16. Voters who remain in the voting booth longer than five minutes may be imprisoned. (Florida)

17. Sunday whistling is prohibited. (Louisiana)

18. South Carolina citizens are required to carry guns to church.

19. It is illegal for any chicken to cross the road. (Quitman, Georgia)

20. Any moving automobile must follow a man carrying a red flag. (Arkansas)

21. Females may be fined if they phone any man for a date. (Tennessee)

22. Nude tub bathing is illegal. Stop it. (Florida)

19 DISTINCT DIALECTS
SPOKEN IN THE SOUTH
(and you thought you just spoke Southern)

Mountain
Plains
Coastal
Virginia Tidewater
General Southern Lowland
South Carolina Low Country
Cajun (Bougalie)
Creole
Gullah
Gumbo

Carolina Mountain
Alabama-Tennessee Low Country
Northern Piedmont
Southern Piedmont
Atlantic Coastal Plain
Thomaston-Valdosta
New Orleanian
Charlestonian
Conch

MOST POPULAR OUTDOOR ACTIVITIES FOR KIDS IN THE SOUTH

Running through the sprinkler

Water-bombing fire ants

Salting slugs

Tying a string to a june bug

Catching fireflies

Swimming

Shooting off bottle rockets

Stealing watermelons

Dropping watermelons from the roof

Bicycling

Splashing through puddles after a thunderstorm

Climbing trees

Falling out of trees

Exploring

Getting sunburned

Getting into poison ivy

Getting bitten by bugs

9 THINGS ABOUT THE SOUTH THAT TERRIFY YANKEES

1. Gas station mechanics ("Don't let them see our license plate or they'll use an ice pick to punch a hole in the radiator.")

2. Speed traps ("They're run by fat, backwater Southern sheriffs in towns with a one-room jail and a torture room behind the outhouse.")

3. Armadillos ("What the hell is that thing? Look out—It's coming this way! Don't let it get any closer!")

4. Fire ants ("What do you mean, 'watch out for the ant hill'? Why should I worry about a little, old—yeoooowwwwww!!!!")

5. Unshaven countryfolk in overalls ("He's just staring at us and doesn't—say—a—word.")

6. Spanish moss ("Could be hiding snakes or lizards." Actually hiding redbugs.)

7. Palmetto bugs ("Yeeeaaaaarrrgggghhh! Get it out of the suitcase!")

8. Kudzu ("How many dead bodies are in there?")

9. Mean, barking hound dogs ("He's just bound to have rabies—look at his eyes!")

10 WAYS TO TAKE IT EASY, SOUTHERN-STYLE

Whittle.

Chew the rag.

Shoot the breeze.

Rest your eyes.

Don't work if you can just piddle.

Don't play if you can just fiddle.

Don't run if you can take it at a walk.

Don't walk if you can just mosey.

Don't mosey if you can just stand around.

Don't just stand there if you can sit down.

Don't just sit there if you can lie down.

VERTICAL LOAFING

HORIZONTAL LOAFING

9 THINGS YOU CAN SHOOT AT ANYTIME IN THE SOUTH

1. GROUND HOG

2. SQUIRREL

3. RABBIT

4. SNAKE

5. COON

6. POSSUM

7. ARMADILLO

8. SNAPPING TURTLE

9. ROAD SIGNS

9 RULES OF SOUTHERN COOKING

1. Cook everything 'til well done and then some.

2. Whenever and with whatever possible, fry.

3. Don't start measurin' ingredients and gettin' all fired up over gettin' a recipe just so. Southern cookin' is done by taste, not by book.

4. When possible, cook with cast-iron skillets and pots for extra flavor.

5. Always have biscuits or some form of soppin' bread with every meal.

6. Always cook more than you can eat, in case company stops by.

7. Don't toss out your grease. Keep a can on the stove for all your drippin's.

8. Don't waste anything.

9. The more you grow, catch, or shoot your own food, the better it will taste.

20 LIP-SMACKIN' EXAMPLES OF TYPICAL SOUTHERN HOME-COOKED EATIN'

BREAKFAST

1. Buttermilk biscuits and gravy, fried eggs and sausage, and 'taters, grits, coffee, and milk

2. Cereal and juice

3. A Moon Pie and a Diet Coke

DINNER (KNOWN UP NORTH AS "LUNCH")

4. Spam (sliced or spread) on white bread, chips, Mountain Dew, and a Goo-Goo Cluster

5. Bologna sandwich on white bread with Miracle Whip, Golden Flake Cheez Curls, and an RC

6. Vienna (pronounced *vy-eena*) Sausages, crackers, a tomato (uncut, eaten like an apple), and a Diet Coke

SUPPER (ICED TEA AND MILK GOES WITH EVERY ONE OF THESE)

7. Buttermilk biscuits and cream gravy, fried chicken, smashed 'taters, corn on the cob

8. Corn pone, fried okra, barbecued anything, greens, and fried 'taters

9. Chicken-fried steak, green beans, creamed corn, sliced tomatoes, and homemade bread

10. Catfish, hush puppies, and cole slaw

11. Pinto beans, ham hocks, and corn bread

12. Fried meat (any kind) 'n' eggs

13. (for lighter appetites) Corn bread and buttermilk (mushed up together in a cereal bowl)

DESSERT

14. Fried pies (peach, cherry, or apple)

15. Cobbler (blackberry, peach, or gooseberry)

16. Strawberries and ice cream

MIDNIGHT SNACKS

17. Graham crackers and milk all mushed up in a glass

18. leftover fried chicken

19. bologna sandwich

20. Cheerios

FOODS ONLY A TRUE SOUTHERNER WOULD EAT
(and even then, not all of us would)

1. okra (fried, yes; boiled, no)
2. blackstrap molasses
3. poke salad
4. collard greens
5. chitlins
6. squirrel
7. possum
8. swamp rabbit
9. coon
10. cooter (turtle)
11. pickled pigs' feet
12. calf/lamb fries (don't ask)

15 CHARACTERISTICS OF A GOOD SOUTHERN "DOWN-HOME" RESTAURANT

1. twice as many booths as tables

2. stools and counter in front of the kitchen

3. menus in plastic covers with a "Today's Special" card paper-clipped on them

4. melmac plates

5. iced tea and water in bumpy plastic tumblers (red or brown)

6. toothpicks at the check-out or (even better) at your table in little jars

TODAYS SPECIAL

CHICKEN FRIED STEAK
MASHED POTATOES, FRIED
OKRA, CORN AND ROLL
$4.95

7. breakfast anytime, day or night (which you'll get grits with, no matter what it was you ordered)

8. plenty of good-natured banter between you and your waitress

9. your choice of cole slaw, salad, or Jell-O salad

10. meat (usually fried) with your choice of three or more vegetables, corn bread, or rolls

11. iced tea, not hot tea

12. jet-black coffee

13. waitresses, not waiters

14. a goodly selection of pies and cobblers for dessert

15. lots of other folks eatin', too

SOUTHERN-BORN SOFT DRINKS
(to wet your whistle and pour your peanuts in)

Ale-8-One, Winchester, KY

Barq's Root Beer, Biloxi, MS

Big Red, Waco, TX

Cheerwine, Salisbury, NC

Coca-Cola, Atlanta, GA

Dr. Pepper, Waco, TX

Jumbo Orange, Chattanooga, TN

Nehi Grape and Orange, Columbus, GA

Pepsi-Cola, New Bern, NC

RC Cola, Columbus, GA

SOUTHERN-BORN JUNK FOOD
(or "Junk Food with Soul")

Elmer's Gold Brick Candy, New Orleans, LA

Goo Goos, Nashville, TN

Golden Flake Potato Chips and Cheez Curls and Corn Chips, etc., Birmingham, AL

Moon Pies, Chattanooga, TN

Nabs, Charlotte, NC

Planters' Peanuts, Suffolk, VA

Slim Jim beef sticks, Raleigh, NC

Zapp's Potato Chips, Gonzales, LA

Fritos, San Antonio, TX

TOP TASTES OF THE SOUTH
(Southern gifts to taste buds throughout the world)

1. honeysuckle
2. Southern-fried chicken
3. Moon Pies
4. Coca-Cola (in 6½-oz. bottles)
5. peanuts in the above
6. Vidalia onions
7. gumbo

8. catfish

9. crawfish

10. shrimp

11. barbecue

12. country ham

13. biscuits and gravy

14. boiled peanuts

15. fruitcake

16. bourbon balls

17. Tabasco Sauce

18. chicken-fried steak

"BOILED, ROASTED, OR IN AN RC
GOOBERS ARE THE SNACK FOR ME"

10 SOUTHERN FOODS THAT MYSTIFY THOSE-NOT-FROM-HERE

Barefoot Bread . . . .(corn pone)
Bosun Bread . . . .(large, flat loaf of bread)
Burgoo . . . .(a barbecued mutton stew)
Chitlins . . . .(fried pig intestines)
Fandaddies . . . .(fried clams)
Frogmore Stew . . . .(seafood stew, no frogs)
Hoppin' John . . . .(black-eyed peas and rice)
Hush Puppies . . . .(corn balls, deep fried)
Limping Susan . . . .(rice and okra)
Snickerdoodles . . . .(cinnamon cookies)
Spoon Bread . . . .(corn bread pudding)

MOST POPULAR PIES OF THE SOUTH

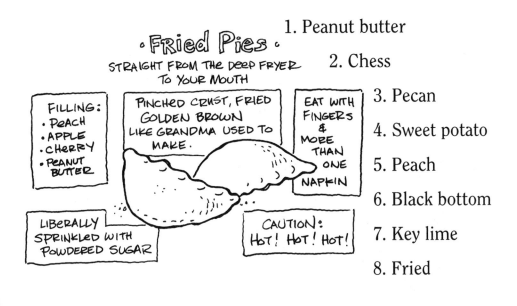

· Fried Pies ·
STRAIGHT FROM THE DEEP FRYER
TO YOUR MOUTH

FILLING:
· PEACH
· APPLE
· CHERRY
· PEANUT BUTTER

PINCHED CRUST, FRIED
GOLDEN BROWN
LIKE GRANDMA USED TO
MAKE.

EAT WITH
FINGERS
&
MORE
THAN
ONE
NAPKIN

LIBERALLY
SPRINKLED WITH
POWDERED SUGAR

CAUTION:
HOT! HOT! HOT!

1. Peanut butter

2. Chess

3. Pecan

4. Sweet potato

5. Peach

6. Black bottom

7. Key lime

8. Fried

17 THINGS TO DO ON A FRONT PORCH

1. swing • 2. shell butterbeans

3. fan yourself • 4. gossip with neighbors

5. gossip about neighbors • 6. drink iced tea

7. read the paper • 8. entertain beaus • 9. cool off

10. eat watermelon • 11. pass along family stories

12. catch june bugs • 13. snooze

14. wave to passersby •15. digest your supper

16. sit and wait for company to arrive

17. say your good-byes

HOW TO GIVE DIRECTIONS, SOUTHERN-STYLE

a right fur piece
down yonder
catty corner
ov' 'air
up 'air
up yonder
thataway

within spittin' distance
back 'air
down 'air
pert' near
just down the road a piece

MOST IMPORTANT SOUTHERN TABLE MANNERS

1. Always say grace before you begin the meal.

2. Pass to the right.

3. Keep your elbows off the table.

4. Use your napkin, not your sleeve.

5. Ladies always leave some of their food uneaten.

6. Toothpicks are appropriate, belching is not.

7. Never ignore someone else's request to pass the food across the table.

8. Ask for seconds whenever possible.

9. Compliment the cook more than once.

THINGS SOUTHERNERS LAUGH AT

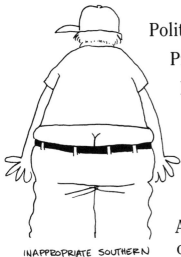

INAPPROPRIATE SOUTHERN
AIR CONDITIONING
(NEVERTHELESS, COMMON)

Politican jokes

Preacher jokes

Redneck jokes

Yankees

Southerners

Uppity folks getting their comeuppance

Accents ("theirs," not our Southern ones)

THE SOUTH ON TV

6 SHOWS THAT GAVE US THE SOUTH AS IT NEVER WAS

"Hee Haw"

"The Dukes of Hazzard"

"Beverly Hillbillies"

"Petticoat Junction"

"Green Acres"

"Real McCoys"

TYPICAL SOUTHERNER'S T.V. SET:

☆ Either one or the other

TV, CD & VCR ALL IN ONE UNIT

RABBIT EARS ANTENNA

TINFOIL TO IMPROVE RECEPTION

19" COLOR SCREEN (PEOPLE LOOK BRIGHT RED)

BROKEN TUNING KNOB

PLIERS TO TURN KNOB WITH

TV GUIDE

48" OR LARGER SCREEN

SATELLITE CONNECTOR

DETACHABLE SPEAKERS USUALLY REMAIN BESIDE TV TO PROVIDE MAXIMUM PROJECTILE AUDIO

VHS TAPE LIBRARY:
· SMOKEY & THE BANDIT
· WRESTLE-MANIA
· 6-HR. CARTOON TAPES
· ETC.

REMOTE CONTROL WITH BUTTONS NO ONE HAS BEEN ABLE TO FIGURE OUT

☆ IN BOTH CASES, THE FOCAL POINT OF THE ROOM AND HOME. (EXCEPTING ONLY THE DINNER TABLE.)

AND 7 THAT GOT IT RIGHT

"The Andy Griffith Show"

"Designing Women"

"Frank's Place"

"In the Heat of the Night"

"Miami Vice"

"Sunrise Sermonette"

"The AM Farm Market Report"

TV SHOWS ANY TRUE SOUTHERNER WILL WATCH ANYTIME

"Gunsmoke"

"The Andy Griffith Show"

"Bonanza"

Stock car races

Football (any kind)

The Kentucky Derby

The weather

SOUTHERN WAYS TO SAY "THANK-YOU"
(because in the South, a simple "thank-you" is never enough)

"Thank-you kindly."

"Bless your heart."

"Bless you, child."

"Much obliged."

"Sure do 'preciate it."

"That's might nice of you."

"Why, you're so sweet to think of me."

11 CHARACTERISTICS
OF SOUTHERN SPEECH
("The closest thang on God's green earth to the King's natchul English"—Anonymous)

As slow enunciation as possible: "Welllllll . . . lemme chew on that a spell."

Gliding (dipthonged) vowels: "Why, yay-yis (yes)!"

Final consonants are often weakened: "Martha, hep (help), yore po' (poor) mama scrub that flo' (floor)."

Accent usually falls on the first syllable: "Yep, the PO-lice caught ol' Bubba last JU-ly."

Added "r"s: "You'd better warsh them clothes before they get up and walk off themselves."

Double modal construction: "I might could do that."

Added "a" at the beginning of words: "I'm said I'm a-gonna do that."

Use of the word "done" for emphasis: "I done did that."

Some words contain added syllables: "My ar-thur-itis is hurtin' something fee-irce."

And some words contain fewer syllables: "You shore do look turrble, all right." or "Git yore tars off my flars." (get your tires off my flowers)

Words ending in "-ed" are pronounced with a final "t": "He ruint my best dress."

10 CHARACTERISTICS OF THE CLASSIC SOUTHERN PICKUP TRUCK

1. Rarely washed, never totally clean

2. Always travels below the speed limit unless on a dirt road

3. No camper shell or bed liner

4. Truck bed often contains: bale of hay, baling wire, empty oil cans, cinder blocks, old tire, rusted tools, rope, chain, ½ of a jack, and one or more ugly dogs

5. Truck body carries two or more good-sized dents: very intimidating to small cars, which usually give it a wide berth

6. Gun rack on rear window containing one or more of the following: shotgun, umbrella, whip, cattle prod, baseball bat, or cowboy hat

7. Muffler that rarely muffles anything

8. Accessories: ball trailer hitch, mud flaps, running board, running lights, and fuzzy dice on the rearview mirror

9. Styrofoam cup on dashboard for spitting tobacco

10. No carpet on floor (especially when this is the preferred spitting target)

DOG

11 TYPICAL SOUTHERN BUMPER STICKERS

I brake for road kill

My son got time off for good behavior

Yankee go home

Cow chips happen

My other car is a John Deere

A wife's place is at the mall

Pass at your own risk: Driver Chews Tobacco

Have You Hugged Your Truck Today?

People Who Want to Outlaw Guns Ought to be Shot

I Don't Care How You Did It Up North

American by Birth, Southern by the Grace of God

SONGS ANY TRUE SOUTHERNER CAN IDENTIFY IN THE FIRST FIVE NOTES
(and can sing 'em, too)

1. "Dixie"

2. "Amazing Grace"

3. "Swing Low, Sweet Chariot"

4. "Ol' Man River"

5. "The Andy Griffith Show" theme song

6. "Zip-a-dee-doo-dah"

7. "Just As I Am"

PHRASES NEARLY EVERY SOUTHERNER USES

1. Smack dab: "There was a big ol' palmetto bug smack dab in the middle of my plate."

2. Holler at me: "Holler at me down at the garage if you need anything."

3. Fixing to: "I'm fixing to go down to the store. Need anything?"

4. Right pretty: "She's a right pretty gal all right."

5. Might could: "I might could fix your car if you'd reach me my tools."

6. "T'weren't nothing"—the correct answer to any compliment given to you.

7. Sho' nuff: "I'm sho' nuff tired of them leftovers."

8. Fired up: "He's all fired up because his boss chewed him out."

9. I reckon: "I reckon I'll just fix me up a snack."

10. "Who drank the last Diet Coke?"

HOW TO MAKE A SOUTHERNER MAD

Make fun of his hat.

Make fun of his truck.

Make fun of his dog.

Try to take away his guns.

Drive faster than he does.

Brag on how much you earn.

Brag on how well your golf game's going.

Mention how little in taxes you had to pay this year.

Complain about tobacco farmers.

Ask him why he talks so funny.

Try to hurry him up.

Ask to borrow his tools.

Complain about the cooking.

Let your dog loose in the neighborhood.

Explain how your local politicians are doing a great job.

Unplug his satellite dish.

Plant kudzu in his garden.

THINGS ALMOST EVERY
SOUTHERNER HAS DONE
(at one time or another)

1. Driven around with the air conditioner on and the windows rolled down.

2. Picked up a snake.

3. Caught a crawfish with his bare hands.

4. Lied to a Northerner about eating chitlins.

5. Actually eaten a peanut butter and mayonnaise sandwich.

6. Sat on a porch at night and listened to family stories.

7. Been bored to death by those same old stories.

8. Gone on a snipe hunt.

9. Taken others on a Snipe hunt.

10. Gone to church on a Wednesday.

11. Cranked homemade ice cream.

12. Salted a slug.

13. Cussed at fire ants.

14. Square danced.

15. Watched a tobacco-spitting contest.

16. Gotten too close to a tobacco-spitting contest.

17. Learned to fry chicken so it's crispy on the outside, juicy and tender on the inside.

18. Fixed a flat tire.

19. Made sun tea.

20. Said "hey" to a stranger on the street who he made eye contact with.

THINGS MOST SOUTHERNERS HAVE PROBABLY NEVER DONE
(and don't intend to do)

1. Snow-skied
2. Traveled to another country
3. Ridden on a subway
4. Said "youse guys"
5. Skipped breakfast
6. Made fun of someone's dog
7. Hunted on horseback
8. Worn a string tie
9. Been in a building over 10 stories tall.
10. Lived anywhere else
11. Called their mama anything but "Mama" and their daddy anything but "Daddy"

BASIC ITEMS IN EVERY SOUTHERNER'S WARDROBE

several gimme caps

cowboy hat

straw hat

overalls

old seersucker suit

blue jeans

belt with silver buckle

cowboy boots

sandals

white socks

"GIMME" CAP

4 TRIED-AND-TRUE METHODS OF CATCHING CATFISH

Dip a line: If you got plenty of time, pull out your old fishin' pole, bobber, hook, and a big ol' fat worm, pull your cap down over your eyes, and hunker down for a nap.

Juggin': Tie an old milk or bleach jug to each end of a fishing line with plenty of hooks on it. Bait your hooks with minnows or leftover chicken gizzards and add a weight to keep your line under the water, then go on about your business. Check your line daily to retrieve your catch and toss back the undesirables (carp, weeds, ol' boots, etc.)

Noodlin': This involves sneakin' up on a catfish snoozing in an underwater log or thicket, grabbing him by the mouth, and wrestling him to land. For the stout of heart only.

Telephonin': This method of fishin' for cat (also known as "crankin'") uses the insides of an old crank telephone to send an electric shock through the water, causing the catfish to float conveniently to the surface for pick up. Downright illegal.

10 BELIEFS MOST SOUTHERNERS HAVE REGARDING "THE NORTH"

1. Be leery of *anybody* hailing from north of the Mason-Dixon Line.

2. Winter lasts at least 8 or 10 months of the year up north, and growing season at best is only 3 or 4 weeks long.

3. Everything there costs too much.

4. Any male hailing from a Northern city is either a mugger, a con man, or a member of the Mafia.

5. There's no such thing as a next-door neighbor in the North, as Yankees live in huge apartment buildings on top of each other.

6. The only pets up north are guard dogs and rats.

7. Yankees ain't got no use for Southerners.

8. We ain't got no use for them, either.

9. Yankees talk funnier than we do.

10. Practically every Yankee will move down south, given the facts or come retirement time.

HOW TO BE A SOUTHERN WRITER
IN 10 EASY STEPS

1. Grow up in the South.

2. Pay attention to everything:
   sights, sounds, smells,
   gossip, eccentricities, etc.

3. Resent being misunderstood by your
   family and vow that you'll show
   them all some day.

4. Stay up 'til all hours of the night
   writing longhand on a legal pad.
   Simultaneously consume large quantities
   of iced tea.

5. Write about Southern things: food, football, insects, insanity, truth, beauty, etc.

6. Be introspective, moody, and distant.

7. Leave home (but write back for money).

8. Get a job and on weekends write a Pulitzer Prize-winning novel psychoanalyzing your hometown and dysfunctional family.

9. Become rich and famous and purchase an antebellum mansion, a satellite dish, and a new pickup truck with a portion of your earnings.

10. Go back and visit your hometown, where folks will ask you when you are ever going to settle down and do something with your life.

ABSOLUTELY NECESSARY ITEMS
IN THE SOUTH

1. screen doors
2. the garden
3. good manners
4. family
5. football
6. church
7. the Bible
8. biscuits

FRIENDLY WELCOME MAT

BIBLE

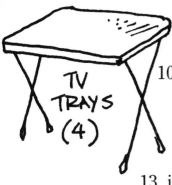

TV TRAYS (4)

9. TV trays

10. a front porch and/or deck

11. a window air conditioning unit

12. fans

13. insect repellent

14. a subscription to *Southern Living*

BOX of OLD GOSPEL & COUNTRY ALBUMS & 8 TRACKS

SOUTHERN LIVING MAGAZINES

9 WAYS A TRAVELER CAN TELL HE IS IN THE SOUTH

1. Grits and biscuits are served with his breakfast, even though he didn't ask for them.

2. The waitress says, "Y'all come back now, honey bun."

3. Rebel flags are available at the gift shop.

4. People in oncoming cars wave at him.

Dixiephobia: unfounded fear of travelling in the south — commonly experienced by Yankees.

5. He drives through clouds of love bugs.

6. He sees Rock City.

7. People listen to him speak, then say, "You ain't from here, are you?"

8. He notes a sharp rise in the number of pickups on the road.

9. Kudzu covers his car while he's at the rest stop.

THE ENEMY
(a roll call of the Southerner's most common adversaries)

palmetto bugs

kudzu

the heat

the humidity

chiggers

ticks

fire ants

raccoons

killer bees

no-see-ums

possums

mosquitoes

mud daubers

snakes

government

politicians

fans of the opposing football team

your lawn

the dog who craps on your lawn

the neighbor with four or more vehicles in his front yard

anyone who makes fun of your hometown and means it

Anyone Not-From-Here

THINGS THAT NORTHERNERS CAN'T UNDERSTAND ABOUT THE SOUTH

1. Peanuts in your RC

2. saying "yessir" and "yes ma'am"

3. grits

4. Beanie-Weenie

5. how to cook a country ham

6. using lard

7. love bugs

8. Southern accents

9. our hospitality

10. how good the food is

11. how the humidity can be so high

12. how it can stay so hot at night

13. why we're not all barefoot

14. why they waited so long to visit us

SWING

MOST COMMON LIES
TOLD BY SOUTHERNERS

1. "You're looking mighty pretty today."

2. "What she says don't bother me none."

3. "We would have been to church last Sunday, but one of the kids took sick."

4. In response to a thank-you for a favor bestowed: "Aw, t'weren't nothin'."

5. "Sure, I remember you folks."

6. "That dog can't hunt."

7. "No, I didn't drink the last Diet Coke."

8. "I reckon you know more about it than I do."

9. "Now, don't you go to any trouble for me."

10. "We just got the satellite dish to catch a good ball game now and then."

AND REPLIES TO THE SAME

1. "I didn't just roll into town on no turnip truck."

2. "You can't BS a BSer."

3. "Why, honey, you're just like your mama."

THINGS YOU SEE MORE OF IN THE SOUTH THAN ANYWHERE ELSE

Baptist churches

golf courses

satellite dishes

juke joints

porches with people on 'em

dirt roads

chicken coops

tractors (normally on the road in front of you)

flamingos

tobacco

hound dogs (sleeping)
armadillos (dead on the road)
possums (ditto)
big-hair women
barbecue
headache powders
tornadoes
drive-in movies
drive-in theaters
Bibles
Southern Living magazine
Rock City signs

PLACES YOU CAN STILL FIND THE CLASSIC SOUTHERN FUNERAL FAN

a tent revival

church homecoming potlucks

an all-day church sing

political rallies

the front porch

high school graduation

auctions

funeral parlors

PICTURES YOU'LL FIND
ON FUNERAL FANS

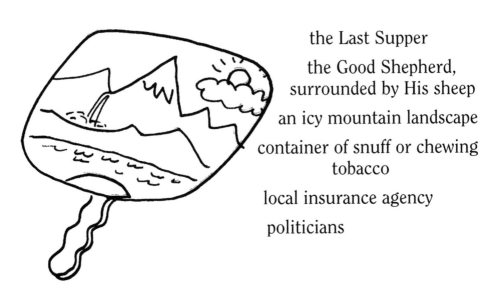

the Last Supper

the Good Shepherd,
surrounded by His sheep

an icy mountain landscape

container of snuff or chewing
tobacco

local insurance agency

politicians

THINGS BELOVED BY SOUTHERNERS

America
(except for the government)

ancestors

land

country music

Elvis Presley

pickup trucks

high school football
games

Scarlett O'Hara

Rhett Butler

the little country church

Goo Goos

RC Cola

our accents

azaleas

people who are "just folks"

the blues

Goo Goo !

duck hunting

flirting

fried pies

home

hospitality

tradition

living at a leisurely pace

pecans

quilts

soul food

potlucks

parades

bluegrass (both kinds)

the Grand Ole Opry

fireworks

tailgating at ballgames

cedar Christmas trees

the beach

magnolia trees

restaurants that serve
breakfast anytime

gospel music

griping about politicians

country ham

hunting

fishing

all-you-can-eat buffets

chicken-fried steak

biscuits

family pictures

good manners

slow talkers

driving fast

loafing

piddling

dinner on the church grounds

watermelon

Vacation Bible School

big hair

baptizing in a creek

afternoon hymn sings

porches

tractors
ugly dogs
barbecue
golf
iced tea
lemonade
Sunday dinner
Confederate flag
watermelon
good ol' boys
"Dixie"

6½-oz. Cokes
Wal-Mart
the church softball team
air conditioning
stock-car racing

Moon Pies
Mama and Daddy
family

A GOOD SOUTHERN HOSTESS KNOWS . . .

not only the fine art of hospitality, but also the art of
reminding you that she is being hospitable.

that in the South, hospitality is never a solo act.
Both hosts and guests conspire to entertain one another.

how to make a guest feel special without feeling intrusive.

that her guest is more important than the food.

how to listen.

when to speak.

how to have a good time, too.

how to pamper you so many different ways, one of 'em is bound to suit.

how to say "good-bye" with grace and tact.

CORNERSTONES OF SOUTHERN HOSPITALITY
(the fine art of making your guests want to stay, without interfering with their departure)

1. ceremony (a flair for the dramatic)

2. personal attention

3. good (but not extravagant) food

10 MOST OFTEN HEARD HYMNS IN THE SOUTH

1. "Amazing Grace"
2. "I'll Fly Away"
3. "Are You Washed in the Blood?"
4. "Nothing But the Blood"
5. "Softly and Tenderly"
6. "The Old Rugged Cross"
7. "Sweet By and By"
8. "I Surrender All"
9. "Bringing in the Sheaves"
10. "Trust and Obey"

LONGEST, MOST FEARED HYMN

"Just As I Am"

THINGS TO DO
AT A SOUTHERN FAMILY REUNION

Get the kids as clean as possible.

Threaten to whollop them if they misbehave.

Take your best dish for the potluck.

Kiss people.

Hug people.

Wonder at all the babies.

Wonder who those people are over there.

Pretend you know everybody's name, even when you haven't a clue.

Note who's put on weight.

Note who's balding.

Note who's not there.

Eat.

Catch up on the latest family gossip (mainly centered on those family members not in attendance).

Look at your cousins' family pictures.

Pose for the family reunion picture.

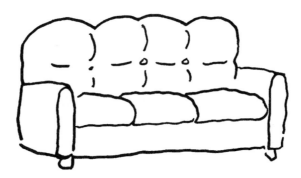

Think how everyone is getting so old.

Wonder if you're getting old.

Resume the same conversation you began with your cousin at the last reunion.

Pitch horseshoes.

Take pictures.

Miss your great-grandma.

Fuss at your kids for getting so dirty.

Eat again.

Continue process 'til dark.

SOUTHERN NAMES FOR NAMESAKES
(when just one of you isn't enough)

Example: Father's name is Odell.

MALE NAMESAKES:

Li'l Odell

Odell Jr. (*never* Odell II)

FEMALE NAMESAKES:

Odella

Odellina

Odelva

A SELECTION OF GOOD SOUTHERN NAMES: MEN

Norris	Dewey
Cletus	Cloyd
Buford	Gaylen
Bubba	Odell
Virgil	Lyndall
Otho	Gerl
Emmett	Dewayne
Dub	Kermit
Rebel	

WHEN ONE NAME JUST AIN'T ENOUGH, TWO FIT, TOO

Bobby Joe	Jim Bob
Billy Ed	Willie Lee
Sammy Ray	

WHEN ONE NAME IS PLAIN TOO MUCH, USE JUST INITIALS:

J. R.	L. A.
R. B.	H. P.

No one'll ask what the initials stand for—they're just accepted as is.

A SELECTION OF GOOD SOUTHERN NAMES: WOMEN

Beulah LaDawn

LaVerne Eula

Rebella Lurline

Joetta Ozelle

Bettina Starla

Inabell Zelma

WHEN ONE NAME AIN'T ENOUGH, TWO FIT, TOO:

Julie May   Ora Lee
Bobbie Jo   Ida Sue
Dora Mae

A FEW GOOD SOUTHERN PROVERBS TO CHEW ON

Your dog is the only thing in the world that loves you more than you love yourself.

The South is the only place left that doesn't need explainin'.

You can always fit into those pants one more time.

You better eat your beans.

Others first, yourself last.

Blood is thicker than brains.

A Southern gentleman is one who always rises when his wife brings in the firewood.

Temptation is the mother of invention.

The most likely time someone will start talking about a relative who died while eating dinner is in the middle of dinner.

Hard work is the mama of good luck.

The best sermon is lived, not preached.

No Southerner can resist a lost cause.

You can see the dead rise every Sunday—when the preacher dismisses the service.

You can only hate what threatens you.

Being American is incidental—being Southern's to the bone.

15 THINGS A TRUE SOUTHERNER KNOWS

1. The difference between a hissie fit and a conniption fit.

2. Pretty much how many fish make up a mess.

3. What general direction cattywampus is.

4. That "gimme sugar" don't mean pass the sugar.

5. When "by and by" is.

6. How to handle their "pot likker."

ALWAYS FLEE IN THE FACE OF A FOOT STOMPIN', SNOT SLINGIN' ROYAL HISSIE FIT.

7. The best gesture of solace for a neighbor who's got trouble is a plate of cold potato salad.

8. The difference betweeen "pert' near" and "a right far piece."

9. When you say, "Come back," you really mean, "Go away."

10. The difference between a redneck, a good ol' boy, and po' white trash.

11. Never to go snipe hunting twice.

12. Never to assume that the other car with the flashing turn signal is actually going to make a turn.

13. You may wear long sleeves, but you should always roll 'em up past the elbows.

14. You should never loan your tools, pickup, or gun to nobody.

15. The South's more American than America.

YOUR TURN: STUFF I MISSED
(that anybody with a lick of sense knows should've been in this book)

Write it down. Tell me why it should've been in here (but don't have a hissy fit about it). Send it to me at the following address:

Jim Erskine
c/o Pelican Publishing Company
P.O. Box 3110
Gretna, LA 70054

I'll give you a holler if I use your contribution in an upcoming book.